One Small Place by the Sea

By Barbara Brenner

Illustrated by Tom Leonard

HarperCollins Publishers

To Olivia G.
—B.B.

For Rose, who changed my life
—T.L.

One Small Place by the Sea · Text copyright © 2004 by Barbara Brenner · Illustrations copyright © 2004 by Tom Leonard
Manufactured in China by South China Printing Company Ltd. All rights reserved. · www.harperchildrens.com
Library of Congress Cataloging-in-Publication Data · Brenner, Barbara.
One small place by the sea / by Barbara Brenner ; illustrated by Tom Leonard.—1st ed. · p.   cm.
Summary: For one afternoon, a child visitor observes the cycle of change within a tide pool, a small place at the edge of the sea
that is home to many plants and animals.
ISBN 0-688-17182-6 — ISBN 0-688-17183-4 (lib. bdg.) · 1. Tide pool ecology—Juvenile literature.
2. Tide pool animals—Habitat—Juvenile literature.   3. Tide pool plants—Habitat—Juvenile literature   [1. Tide pool ecology.
2. Tide pool animals.   3. Tide pool plants.   4. Ecology.]   I. Leonard, Tom, ill.   II. Title. · QH541.5.S35 B74   2004
577.69'9—dc21   2002001180
Typography by Stephanie Bart-Horvath
1 2 3 4 5 6 7 8 9 10 · ❖ · First Edition

A tide pool.
One small place—
this one's no bigger than a bathtub.
It lies among rocks and weeds
at the edge of the sea.

At high tide it's full of water.
At low tide it's no more than a salty puddle.

Tides make it and unmake it twice a day.
That's where it gets its name—*tide* pool.

Imagine standing at the
rim of this tide pool as
the tide is coming in.

What do you see?

Dozens of small animals
and plants
jumbled together—
over
under
next to
on top of
one another.

After a while your eyes
begin to sort them out.

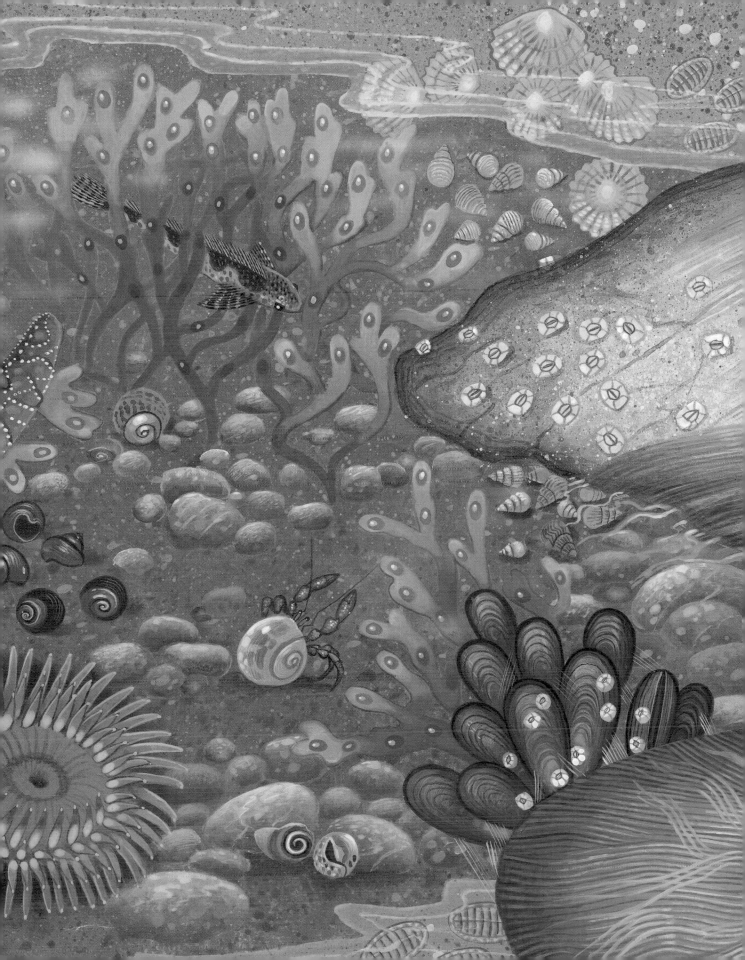

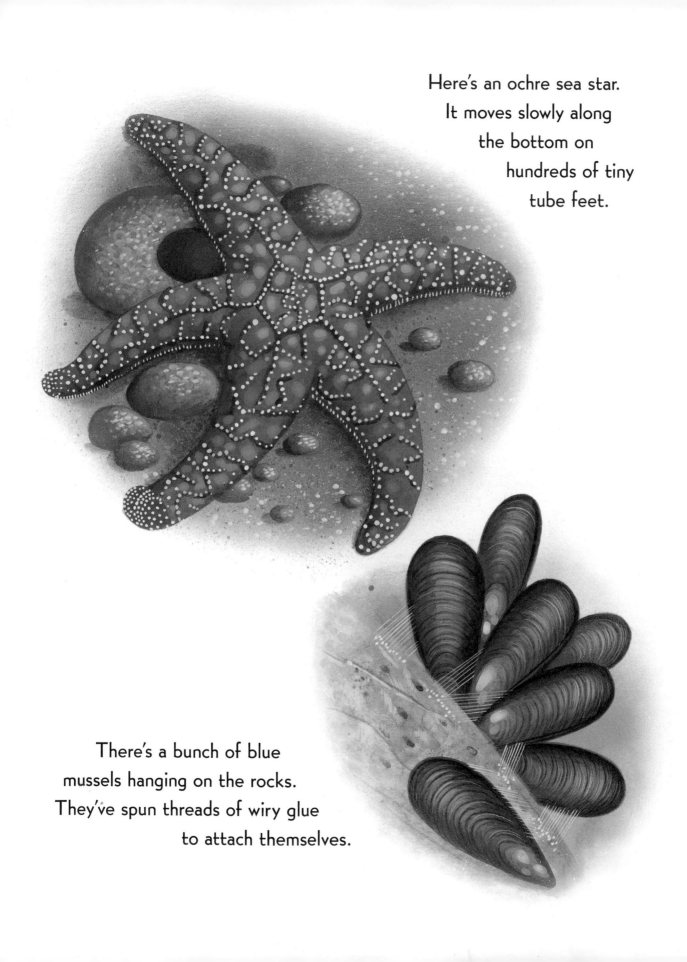

Here's an ochre sea star.
It moves slowly along
the bottom on
hundreds of tiny
tube feet.

There's a bunch of blue
mussels hanging on the rocks.
They've spun threads of wiry glue
to attach themselves.

On the sandy bottom of the pool are two giant green anemones. The anemones *look* like plants. They're really animals.

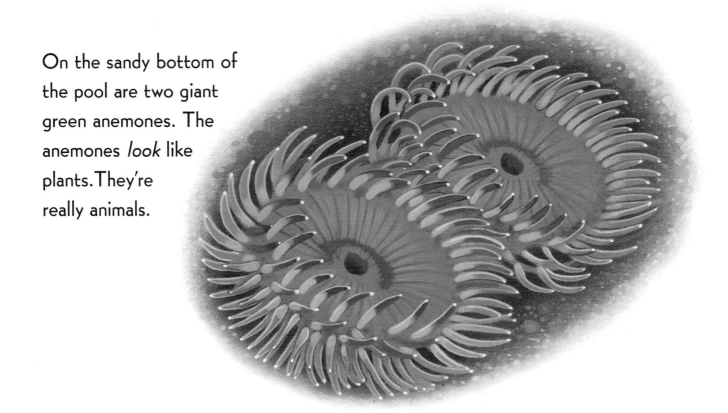

But—that creature in the weeds that looks like a fish— that *is* a fish. It's a sculpin, a fish that lives only in tide pools.

Now you're looking more closely.
You begin to see
smaller and smaller things.
Hermit crabs. Turban snails.
Periwinkles, limpets, chitons,
and a rock covered with barnacles.

You lift a tangle of seaweed.
Surprise! Worms, bugs, and snails
no bigger than a baby's fingernail.

Next you scoop up water in a jar.
You see even smaller creatures.
Hundreds more are in your jar,
but they're too small to see.
You're looking at plankton—
the living "soup" of the sea.

And then—you bend down.
You touch the green leaves of sea lettuce.
You feel the velvety mats of algae.

Now you know what lives in this tide pool.

But what goes on in this small place?

Watch the incoming tide.

The first waves splash over the rim of the tide pool.
Fresh seawater filled with plankton pours in.
Here comes food!

The mussel shells open.
The plankton-filled water spills into the open shells.
The mussels' gills act as strainers—
water out, plankton in.

The barnacles join the plankton feast.
The tops of their shells open.
Out come their legs!
The legs wave like tiny feathers,
kicking bits of food
down inside the barnacle shells
and into their mouths.
Upside-down dinner!

Now the sea star goes hunting.
It climbs up the rocks,
moves among the mussel colony,
picks a target.

The mussel tries to close,
but the sea star pushes itself
inside the mussel's shell.
Its powerful stomach juices
turn the mussel into mush.
The sea star sucks up the mush.

A turban snail glides by.
It picks up the scent of the sea star.
Alarmed, it moves away.
But in its haste it brushes against the tentacles
of one of the anemones.

Those tentacles are deadly.
In a few seconds the snail
is food for the anemone.
It eats the soft parts and
spits out the hard shell.

A hermit crab sees the empty shell.
It looks it over.
This is not about food.
It's about space.
The crab has outgrown
the shell that was its home.

It tries on the empty shell for size.
Good fit!
It will move away, carrying the new
home on its back.

The sculpin swims to the surface
of the tide pool and climbs out.
For a few hours now it will live on air.

Using its front fins as legs,
the sculpin walks on the rocks,
looking for tiny shrimp and sea spiders
the tide brought in.

The periwinkles, limpets, and chitons are grazing too. Their tongues have teeth like little saws. They use them to scrape algae from the rocks and weeds.

Meanwhile, the algae and other plants are making their own food with sun and air and the water in the tide pool.

After about six hours
the tide turns once again.
The waves no longer
reach the tide pool.
The water level in the tide pool
begins to drop.

The mussels close up.
The sea star rests.
The hermit crab retreats
into its new shell.
Periwinkles, limpets, and chitons
move lower on the rocks
to catch some ocean spray.

The sculpin comes back
to the tide pool
and swims toward
the bottom.

The anemones shrink.
Plants stop making their own food.
It's down time at the tide pool
until the tide comes in again.

Nothing in nature lasts forever.
A sea star might eat all the mussels here.
Then there would be empty space in
the tide pool.
New animals and plants would drift
into that empty space.
The tide pool would look different,
and be different.

Or a gull might come by
and gobble up the sea star.
Without the hungry sea star,
the mussel bed might overgrow.
The tide pool would get too crowded.
Some things would get squeezed out.
Some things might die.
The tide pool would still be a tide pool,
but it would change.

There are tide pools all over the world.
No two are exactly the same size.
No two hold exactly the same animals and plants.

But some things are always the same.
Every tide pool in the world depends on tides.
And every tide pool is one small place
that is home for many things.

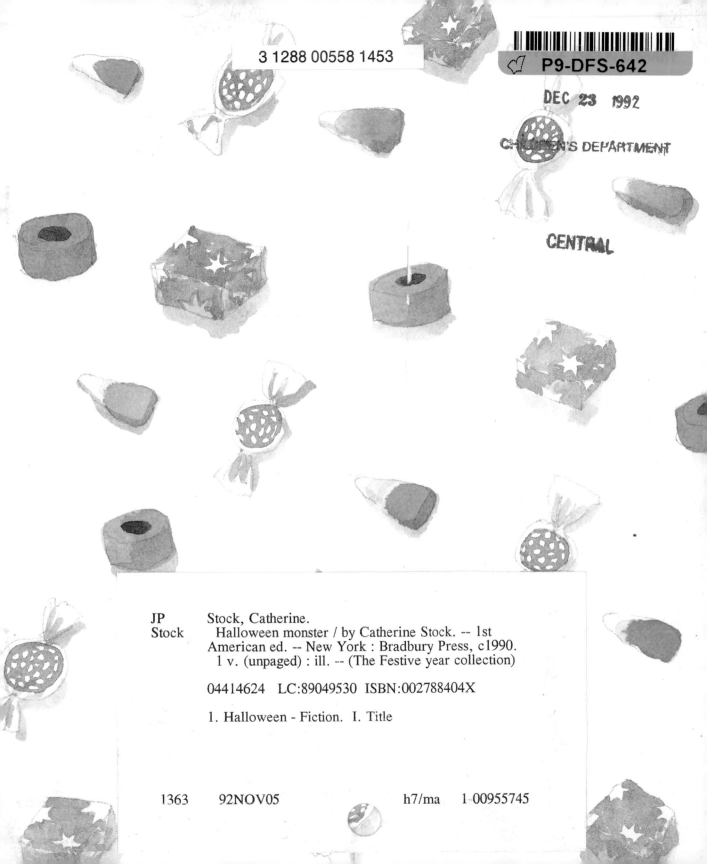

JP   Stock, Catherine.
Stock   Halloween monster / by Catherine Stock. -- 1st
            American ed. -- New York : Bradbury Press, c1990.
            1 v. (unpaged) : ill. -- (The Festive year collection)

            04414624   LC:89049530 ISBN:002788404X

            1. Halloween - Fiction. I. Title

1363   92NOV05   h7/ma   1 00955745

For Adrian

Library of Congress Cataloging-in-Publication Data. Stock,
Catherine. Halloween monster / by Catherine Stock. — 1st ed.
p.   cm. Summary: Tommy is reluctant to dress up and go
out on Halloween until his mother convinces him that
there are no real monsters, ghosts, or witches.
ISBN 0-02-788404-X   [1. Halloween—Fiction.]   I. Title.
PZ7.S8635Hal   1990   [E]—dc20   89-49530   CIP   AC

Halloween Monster

BY CATHERINE STOCK

BRADBURY PRESS · NEW YORK

It's a cold morning. I pull my jacket tight. A gust of wind snatches my cap and whisks it over the fence.

Next door, my friend Billy is helping his dad rake up the leaves. "Come and help us," he calls.

We sweep up all the leaves into a big pile and then we jump into the middle.

We squash the leaves into big plastic bags. Then we have some mugs of cider.

"Halloween is tomorrow," says Billy. "All the monsters and witches and ghosts will be out."

"Want to come trick-or-treating with us, Tommy?" asks his dad.

After lunch we buy some
pumpkins. Billy and I scrape out
all the seeds. Then we draw
faces on the pumpkins for Mom
and Billy's dad to cut out.

Mom roasts the pumpkin seeds with some salt in the oven. They are warm and crunchy.

Billy says that he is going to be a pirate when he goes trick-or-treating. "What about you?" asks Billy.

"Nothing," I say. "I'm not going."

That night, I look under my bed.
No monsters there.

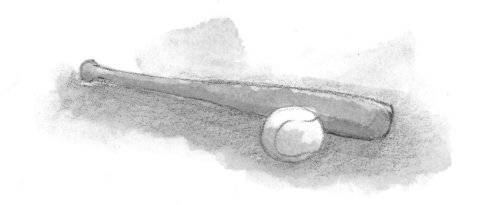

I check the closet.
No ghosts there.

I get under the covers.
Something sits on my bed.
A witch!

I jump up, but it's only Mom.

"I don't want to go trick-or-treating with Billy," I say. "I'm scared of monsters and ghosts and witches."

"There are no monsters or ghosts or witches," Mom says, and kisses me. "Just little children all dressed up."

"Oh," I say.

The next day is Halloween.
Mom makes me a monster suit
with a long tail. Then we make
a mask with big teeth.

Someone's at the door.
   "Trick or treat," shouts a pirate.
   "Grrrraaar!" roars a monster
with a long tail and big teeth.
He gives the pirate some candy
and follows him out the door.

"I thought that you didn't want to come trick-or-treating with us," says the pirate.

"Tommy didn't want to go. But I do," says the monster.